J
597.31   Radlauer, Edward
RAD   Shark mania

Shark
Mania

By Edward Radlauer

AN ELK GROVE BOOK

 CHILDRENS PRESS, CHICAGO

Created by Radlauer Productions, Inc. for Childrens Press

Photographs by Dr. Sheldon Applegate appear
on pages 5, 7, 9, 11, 13, 15, 17, 21, 23, and 32.

Photographs by Jack McKenney of Skin Diver Magazine
appear on pages 19, 25, and 31 and on the book cover.

Photograph on page 27 courtesy of Marineland of the Pacific

Library of Congress Cataloging in Publication Data
Radlauer, Edward.
    Shark mania.

    (Ready, get set, go books)
    "An Elk Grove book."
    SUMMARY: A simple description of sharks' physical
characteristics.
    1.   Sharks—Juvenile literature.   [1.   Sharks]
I.   Title.
QL638.9.R33   597'.31   76-13500
ISBN 0-516-07410-5

10 11 12 13 14 15 R 82 81

Ready, Get Set, Go Books

Ready

Motorcycle Mania
Flying Mania
Skateboard Mania
Shark Mania

Get Set

Fast, Faster, Fastest
Wild Wheels
Racing Numbers

Go

Soap Box Racing
Ready, Get Set, Whoa!
Model Airplanes

Shark mania?

Yes, it's shark mania.

Fins?

A little shark has little fins.

Fins?

A big shark has big fins.

Tail?

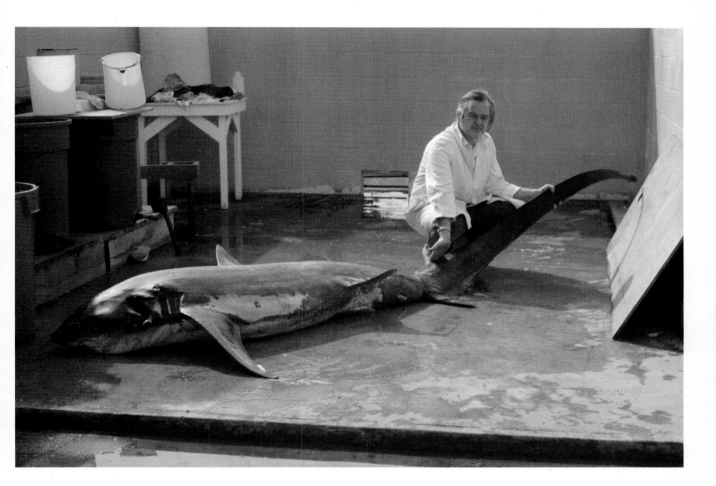

Some sharks have a long tail.

Tail?

This shark has a long tail and a long nose.

13

Nose?

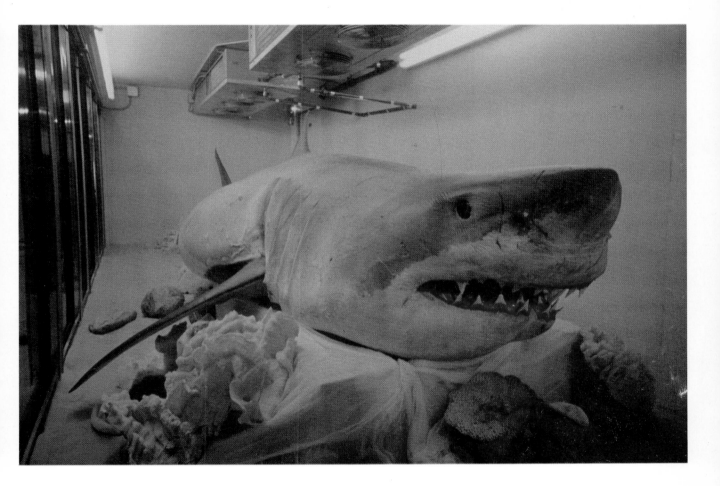

Some sharks have short noses.
All sharks have teeth.

Teeth?

**All sharks have teeth—
sharp teeth.**

Teeth?

Shark jaws are full of sharp teeth.

Jaws?

**A shark from long ago had
very big jaws and big sharp teeth.**

Eyes?

Sharks have very good eyes.

Water?

**All sharks need water—
good clean water.**

Baby shark?

Baby sharks are little.

Fly?

Can this shark fly?

Shark mania?

Yes, it's shark mania.